BOLD KIDS

CHILDREN'S AMERICAN LOCAL HISTORY BOOK

No part of this book may be reproduced or used in any way or form or by any means whether electronic or mechanical, this means that you cannot record or photocopy any material ideas or tips that are provided in this book.
Copyright 2022

All images in this book have been reproduced with the knowledge and prior consent of the artists concerned, and no responsibility is accepted by producer, publisher, or printer for any infringement of copyright or otherwise, arising from the contents of this publication.

Native American tribes lived in Ohio for thousands of years. Before the Revolutionary War, native peoples lived here. The Indians were defeated at the Battle of Fallen Timbers in 1794.

Later, settlers began to farm the land, which was soon transformed into one of the largest producers of glass, machinery, and steel.

In the mid-1800s, the French explorer Robert de La Salle first visited Ohio, bringing with him several settlers from other European countries. The growth of industry led to the influx of laborers from Scandinavia and Central and Southern Europe.

By the Civil War, about half of the population in the state lived in cities. The early twenty-first century, the state's population is still heavily concentrated in urban areas.

The state is rich in wildlife. There are many different kinds of wildlife in Ohio. There are also some interesting facts about the state's history. Columbus discovered the West Indies in 1492, beginning an Age of Exploration in the New World.

In 1670, Robert de La Salle found the Ohio River and established the Ohio Company in Virginia to settle the region. In the late 19th century, the state became a very industrialized and urbanized part of the country. Even today, Ohio is a test-bed for poll trends.

Columbus, the first European to discover the West Indies, began the Age of Exploration in the New World. In 1670, Robert de La Salle mapped the Ohio River and founded the Ohio Company. In 1917, the country enters the French and Indian War.

The Treaty of Paris ceded French land in the New World to the English. In the same year, the American Civil War ends. The Allied forces won the war and the United States became the nation's seventh-most populous state.

The first peoples to settle in Ohio were of European descent. During the early days, many people were of Native American ancestry, while later, white pioneers followed the river valleys and lakeshore. In the nineteenth century, the state was covered by an enormous glacier.

The ice age deposited large amounts of rock, gravel, and other materials that eventually became the state's top industries. During the Civil War, the majority of the population supported the Union, and those who opposed it were called "copperheads."

The state has a rich history. The state is the birthplace of seven U.S. presidents. During the 1800s, a major bridge was built between the United States and Canada. The canalway is the oldest and longest of the three.

Its canal is the most significant waterway in the country. The river was built to connect the Midwest. Throughout history, the state has had a unique history.

The first people to settle in Ohio were European. Historically, there are numerous historical events in the state's history. In 1492, Christopher Columbus landed in the New World and established the first permanent English settlement.

In 1670, Robert de La Salle mapped the Ohio River valley. In 1765, the Ohio Company was formed in Virginia to settle the area. In 1833, the French and Indian War broke out in the state. In 1804, the American Revolution, the Civil War, and the Treaty of Paris ceded the American territories to the English.

In the 1800s, Ohio was covered with hills and river gorges. The state's first white settlers came from New England and Georgia. Many of them were given land grants. Germans, Irish, and Swiss people also settled in Ohio during the mid-1800s.

In the 1920s, the second Ohio Constitution was adopted in Chillicothe. Harriet Beecher Stowe's book, "Uncle Tom's Cabin", depicted the horrors of slavery. The book triggered a civil war and increased tensions between the North and the South.

Milton Keynes UK
Ingram Content Group UK Ltd.
UKHW051046250823
427368UK00008B/60